INTRODUCTION

The story of Em. Z. Svitzers Bjergningsentreprise (Svitzer) begins in 1833 when Emil Zeuthen Svitzer, a Danish entrepreneur, established a salvage business after noticing many losses occurring on trade routes to and from Denmark. Its business extended to harbour towage in due course. Over the last two decades, the company has expanded considerably and claims to have 430 vessels working in about 100 different locations throughout the world.

Svitzer partly joined the huge A P Møller Maersk group in 1973, becoming fully owned in 1982. With takeovers and partnerships, it has expanded rapidly over the last two decades. A significant acquisition in 2006 was Adsteam Marine Ltd which enabled a rapid expansion in Australasia. In 2014, Pacific Basin sold its PB Towage fleet to Smit Lamnalco (SL) and in the middle of the following year Svitzer completed a three-year Service Level Agreement with SL. According to this agreement, Svitzer provides towage services to SL at three major ports in Australia and bareboat charters six of SL's tugs. In 2015 Svitzer acquired a controlling interest in Transmar Serviços Maritimos, a leading tug operator in Brazil.

Because of the huge size of the Svitzer fleet, we are covering it in two volumes. The first volume looked at tugs in the UK and this second volume looks at the company's tugs working in other parts of the world. We begin in Denmark, the home of the company, and move on to other Scandinavian countries and then northern Europe. We look at tugs in Canada, the Caribbean, the Far East and finally Australia where Svitzer has gained prominence as described above. The Australian details start in the north-east of the country and move clockwise.

No guarantee can be given for the accuracy of the data. Different sources provide different figures and we have usually used data provided by *Lloyd's Register*. Modifications are sometimes made by operators and these are not always publicised.

In recent years there have been constant developments in tug design in order to improve power, manoeuvrability and stability while towing, and reference is made in captions as to the propulsion configuration fitted to each tug. Sadly there is insufficient space here to explain the technicalities of Voith-Schneider units, azimuth stern drive (ASD) and tractor tugs. I hope that readers will be encouraged to do their own research on tug propulsion.

Acknowledgements

I wish to thank the many photographers who have made their work available for publication. Sadly it has proved impossible to elicit any help or co-operation from the Svitzer head office in Copenhagen or from local offices. A notable exception is the Western Australia office; otherwise one is left to assume that the company has no interest whatsoever in its fleet, an assumption supported by a failure to maintain an up-to-date website. I also thank my son Dominic for his technical input, and Gil Mayes once again for his proof reading and wise corrections and improvements. Thanks should be recorded to our printers who have once again produced a fine booklet.

Bernard McCall   Portishead   September 2017

Published by Bernard McCall, 400 Nore Road, Portishead, Bristol, BS20 8EZ, England.
Website: www.coastalshipping.co.uk. Telephone/fax: 01275 846178   E-mail: bernard@coastalshipping.co.uk
Printed by Gomer Press, Llandysul Enterprise Park, Llandysul, Ceredigion, Wales, SA44 4JL.   Tel: +44 (0) 1559 362371   Email: sales@gomer.co.uk
ISBN: 978-1-902953-86-1

Front cover : The HASTINGS and TUSKER were photographed at Geelong on 13 December 2007. For tug details, see pages 90 and 92.

(John Nunn)

Back cover : The FENJA, FREYA and FRIGGA on the day of their naming ceremony at Klaipeda on 3 October 1998. The tugs have two 6-cylinder MaK engines with a total output of 4900bhp. They have a bollard pull of 62 tonnes. Most sources claim that these three tugs (and the Svitzer M class) were completed at the Lindø shipyard. This is incorrect, as the image proves.

(Bent Mikkelsen)

Tug: URD
Builder: Limfjordsværft, Aalborg
Engine: 1 x 12-cyl GM Detroit; 700bhp
Propulsion: 1 fixed pitch propeller
Bollard pull: 7.5 tonnes
IMO: --

Year built: 1973

Gross tonnage: 17

Former name(s): GOLIATH IV-98
Later name(s): 07-GOLIAT
Location: Odense, Denmark   Date: 6 July 2006
Comments: Launched by mobile crane

Photographer: Bernard McCall

2

Tug: SVITZER HELIOS

Builder: Asi-Verken, Åmål

Engine: 1 x 16-cyl Nohab; 3200bhp

Propulsion: 1 x controllable pitch propeller

Bollard pull: 35 tonnes

IMO: 7321659

Year built: 1973

Gross tonnage: 304

Former name(s): ARCTIC HELIOS-08, HELIOS-85, VICTORIA-81

Later name(s):

Location: Esbjerg, Denmark   Date: 3 March 2017

Comments:

Photographer: Bent Mikkelsen

Tug: HUGIN

Builder: Aalborg Værft

Engine: 1 x 8-cyl Alpha; 1160bhp

Propulsion: 1 x controllable pitch propeller

Bollard pull: 17 tonnes

IMO: --

Year built: 1980

Gross tonnage: 61

Former name(s): GOLIATH CARL-99, SVAVA-93, GOLIATH RØN-83

Later name(s):

Location: Esbjerg, Denmark   Date: 5 July 2006

Comments:

Photographer: Bernard McCall

Tug: BESTLA

Builder: Dannebrog Værft, Århus

Engine: 1 x 16-cyl B&W Alpha; 2480bhp

Propulsion: 1 x controllable pitch propeller

Bollard pull: 32 tonnes

IMO: 8027779

Year built: 1981

Gross tonnage: 235

Former name(s):

Later name(s):

Location: Copenhagen, Denmark   Date: 22 June 2014

Comments:

Photographer: John Regan

Tug: VØLUND

Builder: Dannebrog Værft, Århus

Engine: 1 x 8-cyl Wärtsilä; 3712bhp

Propulsion: 1 x controllable pitch propeller

Bollard pull: 55 tonnes

IMO: 8131116

Year built: 1983

Gross tonnage: 291

Former name(s):

Later name(s): 06-TROENSE II, 09-VT PROTON

Location: Copenhagen, Denmark   Date: 12 August 2003

Comments:

Photographer: Bernard McCall

Tug: EGIL

Builder: Cochrane, Selby

Engine: 2 x 6-cyl Ruston; 4340bhp

Propulsion: 2 x directional propellers

Bollard pull: 60 tonnes

IMO: 8618334

Year built: 1987

Gross tonnage: 375

Former name(s): STEVNS BUGSER-01, MARIA ISABEL I-98

Later name(s):

Location: Esbjerg, Denmark   Date: 5 July 2006

Comments: Funnels later cut down to improve vision from wheelhouse. In 2017, working in Chiriqui Grande (Panama) area under Panamanian flag.

Photographer: Bernard McCall

Tug: SIGYN
Builder: Svendborg Værft
Engine: 2 x 6-cyl Alpha; 3998bhp
Propulsion: 2 x Z-peller units
Bollard pull: 51 tonnes
IMO: 9114361

Year built: 1996

Gross tonnage: 485

Former name(s):
Later name(s):
Location: Fredericia, Denmark
Comments:

Date: 6 July 2006

Photographer: Bernard McCall

Tug: SVITZER MADEIRA

Builder: Baltijos, Klaipeda

Engine: 2 x 16-cyl Caterpillar; 5710bhp

Propulsion: 2 x directional propellers

Bollard pull: 73 tonnes

IMO: 9292905

Year built: 2005

Gross tonnage: 385

Former name(s): SVITZER MEDEMBLIK-13, SVITZER MULL-09

Later name(s):

Location: Kalundborg, Denmark   Date: 7 July 2017

Comments:

Photographer: Danny Lynch

Tug: SVITZER NANNA   Year built: 2006

Builder: East Isle Shipyard, Georgetown, Canada

Engine: 2 x 16-cyl Caterpillar; 5072bhp

Propulsion: 2 x Z-peller units

Bollard pull: 60 tonnes   Gross tonnage: 381

IMO: 9364368

Former name(s): STEVNS ICECAP-07

Later name(s): 11-FJORD ÉTERNITÉ, 10-STEVNS ICECAP

Location: Copenhagen, Denmark   Date: 7 July 2009

Comments: Working at Port Alfred, Canada, in 2017.

Photographer: David Alcock

Tug: SVITZER GEO   Year built: 2012

Former name(s):

Builder: Baltijos, Klaipeda

Later name(s):

Engine: 3 x 8-cylinder Wärtsilä diesel-electric; 6525bhp

Propulsion: 2 x directional propellers

Location: Fredericia, Denmark   Date: 15 June 2012

Comments: The second of a pair of ECOtugs, reducing fuel consumption
and CO_2 emissions by 10% and NOx emissions by 80%.

Bollard pull: 70 tonnes   Gross tonnage: 433

IMO: 9602459

Photographer: Bent Mikkelsen

Tug: GÖSTA

Builder: Cochrane, Selby

Engine: 1 x 9-cyl Ruston; 2460bhp

Propulsion: 1 x controllable pitch propeller

Bollard pull: 23 tonnes

IMO: 6800438

Year built: 1968

Gross tonnage: 220

Former name(s):

Later name(s): 15-KLINTS, 06-TAK-8, 04-GRIFON-3, 03-TAK-8

Location: Norrköping, Sweden   Date: 28 July 2002

Comments: Röda Bolaget became part of the A P Møller group in 1999 and the Svitzer livery has been gradually applied to the tugs since then.

Photographer: Bernard McCall

Tug: BONDEN

Builder: Asi-Verken, Åmål

Engine: 1 x 6-cyl Pielstick; 3899bhp

Propulsion: 1 x controllable pitch propeller

Bollard pull: 38 tonnes

IMO: 7388669

Year built: 1975

Gross tonnage: 357

Former name(s): HEIMDAL-88, BONDEN-77

Later name(s):

Location: Gothenburg, Sweden   Date: 17 August 2005

Comments:

Photographer: Lennart Ramsvik

Tug: KNUT

Builder: Åsi-Verken, Åmål

Engine: 1 x 16-cyl Allen; 2801bhp

Propulsion: 1 x controllable pitch propeller

Bollard pull: 28 tonnes

IMO: 7407568

Year built: 1976

Gross tonnage: 181

Former name(s): JÄVERÖN-01, VISCARIA-00

Later name(s): 09-CETUS

Location: Norrköping, Sweden   Date: 28 July 2002

Comments: Working in Kokkola, Finland, in 2017.

Photographer: Bernard McCall

14

Tug: BJÖRN AF GÖTEBORG

Builder: Matsuura Tekko, Higashi

Engine: 2 x 8-cyl Yanmar; 4000bhp

Propulsion: 2 x Z-peller units

Bollard pull: 53 tonnes

IMO: 9008665

Year built: 1991

Gross tonnage: 356

Former name(s):

Later name(s): 13-SVITZER BJØRN

Location: Gothenburg, Sweden   Date: 2 September 2003

Comments:

Photographer: Lennart Ramsvik

Tug: BOB
Builder: Moen Slip, Kolvereid
Engine: 2 x 9-cyl Normo; 5160bhp
Propulsion: 2 x Voith Schneider units
Bollard pull: 52 tonnes
IMO: 9155236

Year built: 1997

Gross tonnage: 475

Former name(s):
Later name(s):
Location: Gothenburg, Sweden   Date: 20 July 2006
Comments:

Photographer: Lennart Ramsvik

Tug: SVITZER ODEN

Builder: ASL, Singapore

Engine: 2 x 8-cyl MaK; 7178bhp

Propulsion: 2 x Voith Schneider units

Bollard pull: 70 tonnes

IMO: 9342451

Year built: 2006

Gross tonnage: 670

Former name(s):

Later name(s):

Location: Gothenburg, Sweden   Date: 17 August 2006

Comments:

Photographer: Lennart Ramsvik

Tug: SVITZER MUNIN

Builder: Åsi-Verken, Åmål

Engine: 1 x 6-cyl Pielstick; 3899bhp

Propulsion: 1 x controllable pitch propeller

Bollard pull: 38 tonnes

IMO: 7363970

Year built: 1974

Gross tonnage: 357

Former name(s): DYNAN-04

Later name(s): 08-DYNAN

Location: Tallinn, Estonia   Date: 6 May 2008

Comments: Working in Swedish ports in 2017

Photographer: Jukka Koskimies

Tug: SVITZER VIDAR

Builder: Zamakona, Santurce

Engine: 2 x 8-cylinder Bergens; 6528bhp

Propulsion: 2 x directional propellers

Bollard pull: 80 tonnes

IMO: 9319181

Year built: 2005

Gross tonnage: 386

Former name(s): R CATALUNYA-16

Later name(s):

Location: Bremerhaven, Germany   Date: 29 November 2016

Comments:

Photographer: Drago Krivokapic

Tug: SVITZER ROTA

Builder: Damen Song Cam, Haiphong

Engine: 2 x 16-cyl Caterpillar; 5632bhp

Propulsion: 2 x directional propellers

Bollard pull: 62 tonnes

IMO: 9760859

Year built: 2016

Gross tonnage: 299

Former name(s):

Later name(s):

Location: Bremerhaven, Germany

Comments:

Date: 13 February 2017

Photographer: Poul Erik Olsen

Tug: SVITZER RAN

Builder: Damen Song Cam, Haiphong

Engine: 2 x 16-cyl Caterpillar; 5632bhp

Propulsion: 2 x directional propellers

Bollard pull: 62 tonnes

IMO: 9760847

Year built: 2016

Gross tonnage: 299

Former name(s):

Later name(s):

Location: Bremerhaven, Germany   Date: 6 November 2016

Comments:

Photographer: Poul Erik Olsen

Tug: ROTTERDAM

Builder: De Merwede, Hardinxveld

Engine: 2 x 9-cyl Werkspoor; 13,500bhp

Propulsion: 2 x controllable pitch propellers

Bollard pull: 167 tonnes

IMO: 7402439

Year built: 1975

Gross tonnage: 2708

Former name(s): SMITWIJS ROTTERDAM-07, SMIT ROTTERDAM-98

Later name(s): 13-GLOBAL DESTINY

Location: New Waterway, Netherlands   Date: 27 July 2008

Comments: Arrived Alang for recycling in December 2013 but resold for further trade. Eventually recycled at Gadani Beach in September 2014.

Photographer: Ruud Zegwaard

Tug: FRIESLAND

Builder: Tille, Kootstertille

Engine: 2 x 8-cyl Bolnes; 2400bhp

Propulsion: 2 x Z-peller units

Bollard pull: 35 tonnes

IMO: 8113657

Year built: 1982

Gross tonnage: 234

Former name(s):

Later name(s):

Location: North Sea Canal, Netherlands   Date: 29 May 2006

Comments:

Photographer: Dominic McCall

Tug: SVITZER SVEZIA

Builder: Ferrari, La Spezia

Engine: 2 x 6-cyl Deutz; 3222bhp

Propulsion: 2 x directional propellers

Bollard pull: 40 tonnes

IMO: 8521141

Year built: 1988

Gross tonnage: 245

Former name(s): SVEZIA-14

Later name(s):

Location: North Sea Canal, Netherlands

Comments:

Date: 27 September 2016

Photographer: Ian Willett

Tug: SIMSON

Builder: Santodomingo, Vigo

Engine: 2 x 8-cyl ABC; 4340bhp

Propulsion: 2 x controllable pitch propellers

Bollard pull: 52 tonnes

IMO: 9054365

Year built: 1993

Gross tonnage: 314

Former name(s):

Later name(s):

Location: IJmuiden, Netherlands   Date: 4 August 2003

Comments:

Photographer: Bernard McCall

Tug: TITAN

Builder: Santodomingo, Vigo

Engine: 2 x 8-cyl ABC; 4340bhp

Propulsion: 2 x directional propellers

Bollard pull: 51 tonnes

IMO: 9054353

Year built: 1993

Gross tonnage: 314

Former name(s):

Later name(s): 09-MAIDEN CASTLE

Location: IJmuiden, Netherlands   Date: 29 May 2006

Comments: Based at Portland (UK) in 2017.

Photographer: Dominic McCall

Tug: THETIS

Year built: 2003

Builder: Hull - Dunav, Bezdan; completed - IHC Delta, Sliedrecht

Engine: 2 x 9-cyl Wärtsilä; 4596bhp

Propulsion: 2 x directional propellers

Bollard pull: 65 tonnes

Gross tonnage: 331

IMO: 9252527

Former name(s):

Later name(s):

Location: North Sea Canal, Netherlands   Date: 27 September 2016

Comments: THETIS had been owned by Iskes Towage & Salvage, but in 2014 Iskes joined with Svitzer to form Port Towage Amsterdam.

Photographer: Ian Willett

Tug: SVITZER BUFFEL
Builder: Sanmar, Istanbul
Engine: 2 x 8-cyl Caterpillar; 1100bhp
Propulsion: 2 x fixed pitch propellers
Bollard pull: 30 tonnes
IMO: --

Year built: 2004

Gross tonnage: 78

Former name(s):
Later name(s):
Location: IJmuiden, Netherlands   Date: 21 October 2008
Comments: Working in Dominican Republic in 2017.

Photographer: Richard Potter

Tug: SVITZER MUIDEN

Builder: Baltijos, Klaipeda

Engine: 2 x 6-cyl MaK; 4894bhp

Propulsion: 2 x directional propellers

Bollard pull: 52 tonnes

IMO: 9292888

Year built: 2004

Gross tonnage: 385

Former name(s):

Later name(s):

Location: IJmuiden, Netherlands   Date: 23 June 2008

Comments:

Photographer: Kevin Jones

Tug: SVITZER MARKEN

Builder: Baltijos, Klaipeda

Engine: 2 x 16-cyl Caterpillar; 5710bhp

Propulsion: 2 x directional propellers

Bollard pull: 73 tonnes

IMO: 9292890

Year built: 2005

Gross tonnage: 385

Former name(s):

Later name(s):

Location: IJmuiden, Netherlands   Date: 28 May 2006

Comments: Transferred to Bremerhaven in late December 2013 to launch Svitzer operation there. Still at Bremerhaven in 2017.

Photographer: Dominic McCall

Tug: SVITZER LONDON

Builder: Damen Song Cam, Haiphong

Engine: 2 x 16-cyl Caterpillar; 6772bhp

Propulsion: 2 x directional propellers

Bollard pull: 82 tonnes

IMO: 9695511

Year built: 2014

Gross tonnage: 450

Former name(s):

Later name(s):

Location: Rotterdam, Netherlands   Date: 1 July 2014

Comments: Entered service in Rotterdam; transferred to Gravesend fleet in September 2014.

Photographer: John Regan

Tug: SVITZER TYPHOON

Builder: Damen Shipyard Sharjah

Engine: 2 x 16-cyl Caterpillar; 5706bhp

Propulsion: 2 x directional propellers

Bollard pull: 72 tonnes

IMO: 9780067

Year built: 2017

Gross tonnage: 264

Former name(s):

Later name(s):

Location: North Sea Canal, Netherlands   Date: 3 May 2017

Comments:

Photographer: Willem van der Moolen

Tug: SVITZER LEIXOES

Builder: Tille, Kootstertille

Engine: 2 x 8-cyl Bolnes; 2402bhp

Propulsion: 2 x directional propellers

Bollard pull: 40 tonnes

IMO: 8000848

Year built: 1981

Gross tonnage: 238

Former name(s): GRONINGEN-05

Later name(s):

Location: Lisbon, Portugal   Date: 23 July 2016

Comments:

Photographer: Willem van der Moolen

Tug: SVITZER LISBOA

Builder: Tille, Kootstertille

Engine: 2 x 8-cyl Bolnes; 2400bhp

Propulsion: 2 x Z-peller units

Bollard pull: 40 tonnes

IMO: 8117495

Year built: 1982

Gross tonnage: 238

Former name(s): BRABANT-05, AJAX-99, BRABANT-90

Later name(s):

Location: Lisbon, Portugal   Date: 22 November 2016

Comments:

Photographer: Ventuari

Tug: SVITZER FUNCHAL

Builder: Båtservice, Mandal

Engine: 2 x 8-cyl MaK; 4350bhp

Propulsion: 2 x Z-peller units

Bollard pull: 57 tonnes

IMO: 8714285

Year built: 1988

Gross tonnage: 429

Former name(s): LAVAN-13, SV LAVAN-12, LAVAN-11, TENAX-03

Later name(s):

Location: Lisbon, Portugal   Date: 20 August 2013

Comments:

Photographer: Pedro Amaral

Tug: SVITZER SETUBAL

Builder: Matsuura Tekko, Higashi

Engine: 2 x 6-cyl Yanmar; 4000bhp

Propulsion: 2 x Z-peller units

Bollard pull: 53 tonnes

IMO: 9008653

Year built: 1991

Gross tonnage: 356

Former name(s): LARS-13

Later name(s):

Location: Lisbon, Portugal   Date: 13 March 2017

Comments:

Photographer: Pedro Amaral

Tug: SVITZER PORTIMAO

Builder: Jiangsu, Zhenjiang

Engine: 2 x 6-cyl Niigata; 5000bhp

Propulsion: 2 x Z-peller units

Bollard pull: 70 tonnes

IMO: 9554339

Year built: 2011

Gross tonnage: 442

Former name(s):

Later name(s):

Location: Sines, Portugal   Date: 6 December 2016

Comments:

Photographer: Drago Krivokapic

Tug: SVITZER MONTREAL   Year built: 2004   Former name(s): SVITZER CAUCEDO-16, CAUCEDO-16
Builder: East Isle Shipyard, Georgetown, Canada   Later name(s):
Engine: 2 x 16-cyl Caterpillar; 5072bhp   Location: Montreal, Canada   Date: 11 September 2016
Propulsion: 2 x directional propellers   Comments:
Bollard pull: 64 tonnes   Gross tonnage: 402
IMO: 9295658   Photographer: Richard Clammer

Tug: SVITZER CARTIER

Builder: Shanghai Harbour

Engine: 2 x 6-cyl Yanmar; 5400bhp

Propulsion: 2 x Voith Schneider units

Bollard pull: 56 tonnes

IMO: 8668248

Year built: 2007

Gross tonnage: 350

Former name(s): SVITZER WOMBI-15, HAI GANG 107-14

Later name(s):

Location: Montreal, Canada   Date: 11 September 2016

Comments:

Photographer: Richard Clammer

Tug: BARBADOS II

Year built: 2002

Builder: Hull - SevMash, Severodvinsk; completion - Damen, Gorinchem

Engine: 2 x 6-cyl Caterpillar; 5520bhp

Propulsion: 2 x directional propellers

Bollard pull: 75 tonnes

Gross tonnage: 313

IMO: 9229221

Former name(s):

Later name(s):

Location: Bridgetown, Barbados   Date: 27 November 2015

Comments: In 2015, Svitzer and the Barbados Port Authority signed a 15-year agreement for Svitzer to provide towage services.

Photographer: John Southwood

Tug: PELICAN II   Year built: 1993
Builder: Hull - Stocznia Tczew; completion - Damen Gorinchem
Engine: 2 x 6-cyl Caterpillar; 4704bhp
Propulsion: 2 x fixed pitch propellers
Bollard pull: 40 tonnes   Gross tonnage: 307
IMO: 9044815

Former name(s):
Later name(s):
Location: Bridgetown, Barbados   Date: 20 March 2016
Comments: The tug has always been named PELICAN II despite the
absence of the II on the photograph.
Photographer: Danny Lynch

Tug: NIZAO

Builder: Pirlant Shipyard, Tuzla

Engine: 2 x 12-cyl Caterpillar; 3344bhp

Propulsion: 2 x Z-peller units

Bollard pull: 45 tonnes

IMO: 9433535

Year built: 2009

Gross tonnage: 247

Former name(s): Completed as ULUPINAR IV

Later name(s):

Location: Basseterre, St Kitts   Date: 19 April 2015

Comments:

Photographer: Danny Lynch

Tug: HERCULES

Builder: Zamakona, Santurce

Engine: 2 x 6-cyl Niigata; 4000bhp

Propulsion: 2 x Z-peller units

Bollard pull: 50 tonnes

IMO: 9206920

Year built: 2000

Gross tonnage: 343

Former name(s):

Later name(s):

Location: Basseterre, St Kitts   Date: 16 April 2017

Comments:

Photographer: Danny Lynch

Tug: MALENA

Builder: East Isle, Georgetown, Canada

Engine: 2 x 16-cyl Caterpillar; 5072bhp

Propulsion: 2 x directional propellers

Bollard pull: 64 tonnes

IMO: 9295660

Year built: 2004

Gross tonnage: 402

Former name(s):

Later name(s):

Location: Willemstad, Curaçao   Date: 30 January 2016

Comments:

Photographer: Danny Lynch

Tug: SOCO

Builder: Pirlant Shipyard, Tuzla

Engine: 2 x 12-cyl Caterpillar; 3344bhp

Propulsion: 2 x Z-peller units

Bollard pull: 49 tonnes

IMO: 9570010

Year built: 2010

Gross tonnage: 276

Former name(s): ULUPINAR VIII-10

Later name(s):

Location: Oranjestad, Aruba   Date: 6 April 2017

Comments:

Photographer: Danny Lynch

Tug: SVITZER BEATA

Builder: Damen Song Cam, Haiphong

Engine: 2 x 16-cyl Caterpillar; 5710bhp

Propulsion: 2 x directional propellers

Bollard pull: 65 tonnes

IMO: 9760835

Year built: 2016

Gross tonnage: 299

Former name(s):

Later name(s):

Location: La Romana, Dominican Republic   Date: 13 April 2007

Comments:

Photographer: Danny Lynch

Tug: SVITZER KORSAKOV
Builder: Admiralty Shipyard, St Petersburg
Engine: 2 x 8-cyl Bergens; 6308bhp
Propulsion: 2 x directional propellers
Bollard pull: 70 tonnes
IMO: 9389590

Year built: 2007

Gross tonnage: 663

Former name(s):
Later name(s):
Location: Fredericia, Denmark   Date: 18 December 2007
Comments: One of 6 tugs to serve in far east of Russia. Captured by pirates on delivery voyage. Ship & crew released after ransom payment.
Photographer: Bent Mikkelsen

Tug: SVITZER CELESTE

Builder: Cheoy Lee, Hong Kong

Engine: 2 x 6-cyl Caterpillar; 5030bhp

Propulsion: 2 x directional propellers

Bollard pull: 55 tonnes

IMO: 9070333

Year built: 1993

Gross tonnage: 495

Former name(s): CELESTE-06, SMIT KENANGAN-03

Later name(s): 10-ASL CELESTE

Location: Singapore   Date: 23 June 2008

Comments:

Photographer: John Regan

Tug: RIVERWIJS ROWAN

Builder: ASL Singapore

Engine: 2 x 8-cyl Niigata; 5998bhp

Propulsion: 2 x Z-peller units

Bollard pull: 55 tonnes

IMO: 9070313

Year built: 2012

Gross tonnage: 494

Former name(s):

Later name(s):

Location: Singapore   Date: 29 November 2011

Comments: Photographed during fitting out. Riverwijs was established in the 1990s as a joint venture between Svitzer and Riverside Marine.

Photographer: John Regan

Tug: SVITZER BETA

Builder: Qianjin Shipyard, Qingdao

Engine: 2 x 8-cyl Niigata; 5998bhp

Propulsion: 2 x Z-peller units

Bollard pull: 82 tonnes

IMO: 9592410

Year built: 2011

Gross tonnage: 906

Former name(s):

Later name(s):

Location: Singapore

Comments:

Date: 2 August 2014

Photographer: John Regan

Tug: SVITZER ZAIRE
Builder: Qianjin Shipyard, Qingdao
Engine: 2 x 8-cyl Niigata; 5998bhp
Propulsion: 2 x Z-peller units
Bollard pull: 82 tonnes
IMO: 9581576

Year built: 2011

Gross tonnage: 631

Former name(s):
Later name(s):
Location: Singapore   Date: 25 June 2011
Comments:

Photographer: John Regan

Tug: SVITZER KALLANG
Builder: Qianjin Shipyard, Qingdao
Engine: 2 x 6-cyl Niigata; 4998bhp
Propulsion: 2 x Z-peller units
Bollard pull: 72 tonnes   Gross tonnage: 483
IMO: 9464194

Former name(s):
Later name(s):
Location: Colombo , Sri Lanka   Date: 7 February 2014
Comments: The tug is fitted with razor wire to deter pirates.

Photographer: Bob Scott

Tug: SVITZER HANNE

Builder: Sanmar, Istanbul

Engine: 2 x 12-cyl Caterpillar; 4734bhp

Propulsion: 2 x directional propellers

Bollard pull: 60 tonnes

IMO: 9688609

Year built: 2013

Gross tonnage: 212

Former name(s): BOĞAÇAY II-15

Later name(s):

Location: Freeport, Bahamas

Comments:

Photographer: Bob Scott

Date: 12 March 2017

Tug: PELSAERT

Builder: Ocean Shipyards, Fremantle

Engine: 2 x 12-cyl Caterpillar; 2382bhp

Propulsion: 2 x directional propellers

Bollard pull: 31 tonnes

IMO: 8704133

Year built: 1988

Gross tonnage: 190

Former name(s):

Later name(s):

Location: Cairns, Queensland, Australia   Date: 2 September 2015

Comments:

Photographer: John Regan

Tug: GIRU

Year built: 1991

Builder: Adelaide Ship Construction, Port Adelaide

Engine: 2 x 16-cyl General Motors; 3650bhp

Propulsion: 2 x Z-peller units

Bollard pull: 43 tonnes

Gross tonnage: 308

IMO: 9015644

Former name(s):

Later name(s):

Location: Mourilyan, Queensland, Australia

Date: 30 August 2015

Comments:

Photographer: John Regan

Tug: SVITZER NANA
Builder: Qianjin Shipyard, Qingdao
Engine: 2 x 6-cyl Niigata; 5998bhp
Propulsion: 2 x Z-peller units
Bollard pull: 80 tonnes
IMO: 9581643

Year built: 2012

Gross tonnage: 630

Former name(s):
Later name(s):
Location: Bowen, Queensland, Australia   Date: 21 March 2013
Comments:

Photographer: John Regan

Tug: DENISON

Builder: Carrington Slipways, Newcastle

Engine: 2 x 8-cyl Daihatsu; 3854bhp

Propulsion: 2 x Z-peller units

Bollard pull: 58 tonnes

IMO: 8222549

Year built: 1983

Gross tonnage: 473

Former name(s):

Later name(s):

Location: Bowen, Queensland, Australia   Date: 21 March 2013

Comments:

Photographer: John Regan

Tug: AUSTRAL SALVOR

Builder: Carrington, Newcastle

Engine: 2 x 8-cyl Yanmar; 4800bhp

Propulsion: 2 x directional propellers

Bollard pull: 64 tonnes

IMO: 8501385

Year built: 1986

Gross tonnage: 470

Former name(s):

Later name(s):

Location: Bowen, Queensland, Australia   Date: 21 March 2013

Comments:

Photographer: John Regan

Tug: WONGA

Builder: Tamar Shipbuilding, Launceston

Engine: 2 x 6-cyl Daihatsu; 3600bhp

Propulsion: 2 x Z-peller units

Bollard pull: 45 tonnes

IMO: 8116465

Year built: 1983

Gross tonnage: 427

Former name(s):

Later name(s):

Location: Mackay, Queensland, Australia   Date: 31 July 2011

Comments:

Photographer: John Regan

Tug: BELTANA

Builder: Nanindah, Batan

Engine: 2 x 6-cyl Daihatsu; 4894bhp

Propulsion: 2 x Z-peller units

Bollard pull: 60 tonnes

IMO: 9185633

Year built: 2000

Gross tonnage: 395

Former name(s):

Later name(s):

Location: Gladstone, Queensland, Australia   Date: 21 October 2009

Comments:

Photographer: John Regan

Tug: WILGA

Builder: Ocean Shipyards, Fremantle

Engine: 2 x 6-cyl Daihatsu; 3600bhp

Propulsion: 2 x Z-peller units

Bollard pull: 50 tonnes

IMO: 9018921

Year built: 1991

Gross tonnage: 365

Former name(s):

Later name(s):

Location: Brisbane, Queensland, Australia   Date: 26 October 2009

Comments:

Photographer: John Regan

Tug: SVITZER COLMSLIE

Builder: Damen Song Cam, Haiphong

Engine: 2 x 16-cyl Caterpillar; 5710bhp

Propulsion: 2 x Z-peller units

Bollard pull: 69 tonnes

IMO: 9366885

Year built: 2007

Gross tonnage: 313

Former name(s): ADSTEAM COLAC-07

Later name(s):

Location: Brisbane, Queensland, Australia

Comments:

Date: 9 September 2011

Photographer: John Regan

Tug: MAYFIELD

Builder: Alblas, Hendrk-Ido-Ambacht

Engine: 2 x 18-cyl MAN; 2894bhp

Propulsion: 2 x Voith Schneider units

Bollard pull: 49 tonnes

IMO: 8900660

Year built: 1990

Gross tonnage: 496

Former name(s): R19-94, RADHWA 19-93

Later name(s):

Location: Newcastle, New South Wales, Australia Date: 23 October 2016

Comments:

Photographer: John Regan

Tug: CARRINGTON

Builder: Alblas, Hendrk-Ido-Ambacht

Engine: 2 x 18-cyl MAN; 2894bhp

Propulsion: 2 x Voith Schneider units

Bollard pull: 49 tonnes

IMO: 8900657

Year built: 1990

Gross tonnage: 496

Former name(s): R18-94, RADHWA 18-93

Later name(s):

Location: Newcastle, New South Wales, Australia Date: 23 October 2016

Comments:

Photographer: John Regan

Tug: WICKHAM

Builder: Hull - Jac den Breejen, Hardinxveld; compl - Damen, Gorinchem

Engine: 2 x 18-cyl MAN; 4894bhp

Propulsion: 2 x Voith Schneider units

Bollard pull: 49 tonnes

IMO: 8900672

Year built: 1990

Gross tonnage: 496

Former name(s): R20-94, RADHWA 20-93

Later name(s):

Location: Newcastle, New South Wales, Australia

Date: 15 April 2016

Comments:

Photographer: Roger Hurcombe

Tug: SVITZER GINGA

Builder: Nanindah, Batam

Engine: 2 x 16-cyl Caterpillar; 4584bhp

Propulsion: 2 x Z-peller units

Bollard pull: 55 tonnes

IMO: 9373682

Year built: 2006

Gross tonnage: 355

Former name(s): ADSTEAM GINGA-07

Later name(s):

Location: Newcastle, New South Wales, Australia Date: 19 February 2014

Comments:

Photographer: John Regan

Tug: SVITZER MAITLAND

Builder: Baltiyos, Klaipeda

Engine: 2 x 16-cyl Caterpillar; 5710bhp

Propulsion: 2 x directional propellers

Bollard pull: 71 tonnes

IMO: 9324796

Year built: 2006

Gross tonnage: 285

Former name(s): SVITZER MERCUR-10

Later name(s):

Location: Newcastle, New South Wales, Australia   Date: 20 February 2014

Comments: Left Bremerhaven for Australia on board a heavy lift ship on 12 April 2010.

Photographer: John Regan

Tug: SVITZER MERINGA

Builder: Damen Shipyard, Chang De

Engine: 2 x 16-cyl Caterpillar; 5670bhp

Propulsion: 2 x Z-peller units

Bollard pull: 70 tonnes

IMO: 9357834

Year built: 2006

Gross tonnage: 250

Former name(s): ADSTEAM MERINGA-07

Later name(s):

Location: Newcastle, New South Wales, Australia

Date: 13 April 2016

Comments:

Photographer: Roger Hurcombe

Tug: SVITZER HAMILTON

Builder: Damen Song Cam, Haiphong

Engine: 2 x 16-cyl Caterpillar; 5710bhp

Propulsion: 2 x Z-peller units

Bollard pull: 69 tonnes

IMO: 9366914

Year built: 2007

Gross tonnage: 250

Former name(s): SVITZER KIAMA-07, launched as ADSTEAM KIAMA

Later name(s):

Location: Newcastle, New South Wales, Australia Date: 20 December 2015

Comments:

Photographer: John Regan

Tug: MURRAY

Builder: Damen Song Cam, Haiphong

Engine: 2 x 16-cyl Caterpillar; 5710bhp

Propulsion: 2 x directional propellers

Bollard pull: 68 tonnes

IMO: 9389796

Year built: 2008

Gross tonnage: 313

Former name(s): PB MURRAY-15

Later name(s):

Location: Newcastle, New South Wales, Australia   Date: 20 December 2015

Comments: PB MURRAY was one of six PB Towage tugs bareboat chartered for three years by Svitzer in January 2015.

Photographer: John Regan

Tug: DARLING

Builder: Damen Song Cam, Haiphong

Engine: 2 x 16-cyl Caterpillar; 5684bhp

Propulsion: 2 x Z-peller units

Bollard pull: 68 tonnes

IMO: 9389801

Year built: 2010

Gross tonnage: 298

Former name(s): PB DARLING-15

Later name(s):

Location: Newcastle, New South Wales, Australia   Date: 15 April 2016

Comments: The tug wears the colours of Smit Lamnalco which bought Pacific Basin's tugs (PB Towage) in early 2015.

Photographer: Roger Hurcombe

Tug: SVITZER STOCKTON
Builder: Qianjin Shipyard, Qingdao
Engine: 2 x 6-cyl Niigata; 5998bhp
Propulsion: 2 x Z-peller units
Bollard pull: 80 tonnes
IMO: 9581655

Year built: 2012

Gross tonnage: 630

Former name(s): SVITZER NIXIE-13
Later name(s):
Location: Newcastle, New South Wales, Australia   Date: 7 December 2013
Comments:

Photographer: Roger Hurcombe

Tug: PB PLENTY
Builder: Damen Song Cam, Haiphong
Engine: 2 x 16-cyl Caterpillar, 5678bhp
Propulsion: 2 x directional propellers
Bollard pull: 68 tonnes
IMO: 9530498

Year built: 2010

Gross tonnage: 250

Former name(s):
Later name(s):
Location: Newcastle, New South Wales, Australia   Date: 29 August 2016
Comments: Svitzer has bareboat chartered tugs from Smit Lamnalco since September 2015 but this tug has retained her original name.
Photographer: John Regan

Tug: WOONA

Builder: Tamar Shipbuilding, Launceston
Engine: 2 x 6-cyl Daihatsu; 3600bhp
Propulsion: 2 x Z-peller units
Bollard pull: 45 tonnes
IMO: 8302650

Year built: 1984

Gross tonnage: 427

Former name(s):
Later name(s):
Location: Sydney, New South Wales, Australia   Date: 24 February 2008
Comments:

Photographer: John Regan

Tug: GLOUCESTER
Builder: Carrington Slipways, Newcastle
Engine: 2 x 8-cyl Daihatsu; 3854bhp
Propulsion: 2 x Z-peller units
Bollard pull: 55 tonnes
IMO: 8222551

Year built: 1983

Gross tonnage: 473

Former name(s):
Later name(s):
Location: Sydney, New South Wales, Australia   Date: 17 March 2016
Comments:

Photographer: John Southwood

Tug: SL ENDEAVOUR

Builder: Damen Song Cam, Haiphong

Engine: 2 x 16-cyl Caterpillar; 5684bhp

Propulsion: 2 x directional propellers

Bollard pull: 68 tonnes

IMO: 9530486

Year built: 2010

Gross tonnage: 250

Former name(s): PB ENDEAVOUR-15

Later name(s):

Location: Botany, New South Wales, Australia   Date: 25 October 2016

Comments:

Photographer: John Regan

Tug: BARUNGA

Builder: Damen Shipyard, Chang De

Engine: 2 x 16-cyl Caterpillar; 5670bhp

Propulsion: 2 x Z-peller units

Bollard pull: 68 tonnes

IMO: 9277606

Year built: 2003

Gross tonnage: 243

Former name(s):

Later name(s):

Location: Port Kembla, New South Wales, Australia Date: 9 October 2011

Comments:

Photographer: John Regan

Tug: SVITZER MARLOO

Year built: 2006

Builder: Hull - Hin Lee, Zhuhai; completion - Cheoy Lee, Hong Kong

Engine: 2 x 16-cyl Caterpillar; 5068bhp

Propulsion: 2 x Z-peller units

Bollard pull: 61 tonnes

Gross tonnage: 327

IMO: 9391737

Former name(s): ADSTEAM MARLOO-07

Later name(s):

Location: Port Kembla, New South Wales, Australia   Date: 9 October 2011

Comments: Launched as ADSTEAM SHOTLEY

Photographer: John Regan

78

Tug: BULIMBA

Builder: Carrington Slipways, Newcastle

Engine: 2 x 8-cyl Blackstone; 2440bhp

Propulsion: 2 x fixed pitch propellers

Bollard pull: 41 tonnes

IMO: 7815727

Year built: 1979

Gross tonnage: 265

Former name(s):

Later name(s):

Location: Eden, New South Wales, Australia   Date: 6 October 2014

Comments:

Photographer: John Regan

Tug: WARRINGA

Builder: Tamar Shipbuilding, Launceston

Engine: 2 x 8-cyl Blackstone; 2440bhp

Propulsion: 2 x fixed pitch propellers

Bollard pull: 41 tonnes

IMO: 7508233

Year built: 1977

Gross tonnage: 235

Former name(s):

Later name(s):

Location: Eden, New South Wales, Australia

Comments:

Photographer: Roger Hurcombe

Date: 4 April 2016

Tug: COOMA
Builder: Carrington Slipways, Newcastle
Engine: 2 x 6-cyl Daihatsu; 3802bhp
Propulsion: 2 x directional propellers
Bollard pull: 54 tonnes
IMO: 8222082

Year built: 1983

Gross tonnage: 473

Former name(s):
Later name(s):
Location: Eden, New South Wales, Australia   Date: 4 April 2016
Comments:

Tug: SVITZER OLIVIA

Builder: Australian Shipbuilding, Fremantle

Engine: 2 x 9-cyl Deutz; 4840bhp

Propulsion: 2 x directional propellers

Bollard pull: 50 tonnes

IMO: 8006979

Year built: 1989

Gross tonnage: 470

Former name(s): RIVERWIJS OLIVIA-14, HEARSON COVE-02

Later name(s):

Location: Westernport, Victoria, Australia   Date: 30 October 2016

Comments:

Photographer: John Regan

Tug: GABO
Builder: Carrington Slipways, Newcastle
Engine: 2 x 6-cyl Daihatsu; 3600bhp
Propulsion: 2 x directional propellers
Bollard pull: 48 tonnes
IMO: 8112392

Year built: 1982

Gross tonnage: 598

Former name(s):
Later name(s):
Location: Melbourne, Victoria, Australia
Comments:

Photographer: Roger Hurcombe

Date: 5 January 2017

Tug: SL DAINTREE

Builder: Damen Song Cam, Haiphong

Engine: 2 x 16-cyl Caterpillar; 5684bhp

Propulsion: 2 x directional propellers

Bollard pull: 68 tonnes

IMO: 9530474

Year built: 2010

Gross tonnage: 250

Former name(s):

Later name(s):

Location: Melbourne, Victoria, Australia   Date: 26 September 2015

Comments: Repainted in Svitzer colours apart from the wheelhouse which retained Smit Lamnalco colours at the time.

Photographer: John Regan

Tug: SVITZER MARYSVILLE

Builder: Damen Song Cam, Haiphong

Engine: 2 x 16-cyl Caterpillar; 5710bhp

Propulsion: 2 x directional propellers

Bollard pull: 68 tonnes

IMO: 9540443

Year built: 2011

Gross tonnage: 250

Former name(s):

Later name(s):

Location: Melbourne, Victoria, Australia   Date: 3 December 2016

Comments:

Photographer: Roger Hurcombe

Tug: SVITZER OTWAY

Builder: Ha Long Shipbuilding

Engine: 2 x 16-cylinder Caterpillar; 5632bhp

Propulsion: 2 x directional propellers

Bollard pull: 69 tonnes

IMO: 9679828

Year built: 2014

Gross tonnage: 299

Former name(s):

Later name(s):

Location: Melbourne, Victoria, Australia   Date: 3 December 2016

Comments:

Photographer: Roger Hurcombe

Tug: SVITZER EUREKA
Builder: Damen Song Cam, Haiphong
Engine: 2 x 16-cyl Caterpillar; 5632bhp
Propulsion: 2 x directional propellers
Bollard pull: 62 tonnes
IMO: 9783083

Year built: 2016

Gross tonnage: 299

Former name(s):
Later name(s):
Location: Melbourne, Victoria, Australia
Comments: Her first day in the port.

Date: 10 January 2017

Photographer: Roger Hurcombe

Tug: WISTARI
Builder: Carrington Slipways, Newcastle
Engine: 2 x 6-cyl Daihatsu; 3600bhp
Propulsion: 2 x Z-peller units
Bollard pull: 48 tonnes
IMO: 8112407

Year built: 1982

Gross tonnage: 396

Former name(s): W. J. TROTTER-83
Later name(s):
Location: Geelong, Victoria, Australia
Comments:

Date: 6 March 2013

Photographer: John Nunn

Tug: KUTTABUL

Builder: Australian Shipbuilding, Fremantle

Engine: 2 x 8-cyl Niigata; 4202bhp

Propulsion: 2 x Z-peller units

Bollard pull: 55 tonnes

IMO: 8208660

Year built: 1983

Gross tonnage: 1983

Former name(s):

Later name(s):

Location: Geelong, Victoria, Australia   Date: 30 October 2012

Comments: Sold to Ukraine in 2016 and based in Yuzhnyy; still named KUTTABUL.

Photographer: John Nunn

Tug: HASTINGS

Builder: Carrington Slipways, Newcastle

Engine: 2 x 6-cylinder Daihatsu; 3806bhp

Propulsion: 2 x Z-peller units

Bollard pull: 50 tonnes

IMO: 8222070

Year built: 1983

Gross tonnage: 473

Former name(s):

Later name(s):

Location: Geelong, Victoria, Australia

Comments:

Photographer: John Nunn

Date: 26 January 2015

Tug: TOM TOUGH

Builder: Carrington Slipways, Newcastle

Engine: 2 x 6-cyl Daihatsu; 3600bhp

Propulsion: 2 x Z-peller units

Bollard pull: 52 tonnes

IMO: 8112419

Year built: 1983

Gross tonnage: 396

Former name(s): Launched as HERON

Later name(s):

Location: Geelong, Victoria, Australia   Date: 7 May 2014

Comments:

Photographer: John Nunn

Tug: TUSKER

Builder: Tamar Shipbuilding, Launceston

Engine: 2 x 6-cyl Daihatsu; 3600bhp

Propulsion: 2 x Z-peller units

Bollard pull: 47 tonnes

IMO: 8116453

Year built: 1983

Gross tonnage: 426

Former name(s):

Later name(s):

Location: Geelong, Victoria, Australia   Date: 30 October 2012

Comments:

Photographer: John Nunn

Tug: WANDILLA

Builder: Adelaide Ship Construction, Port Adelaide

Engine: 2 x 8-cyl Daihatsu; 1900bhp

Propulsion: 2 x directional propellers

Bollard pull: 28 tonnes

IMO: 7039153

Year built: 1971

Gross tonnage: 243

Former name(s):

Later name(s):

Location: Adelaide, South Australia   Date: 18 December 2012

Comments: On 29 August 2013, handed over to Tribal Warrior
Association for training young Aboriginal and Torres Strait Islanders.

Photographer: John Regan

Tug: MARIMBA
Builder: Carrington Slipways, Newcastle
Engine: 2 x 8-cyl Blackstone; 2440bhp
Propulsion: 2 x fixed pitch propellers
Bollard pull: 42 tonnes
IMO: 7636004

Year built: 1978

Gross tonnage: 265

Former name(s): CHARLES WAUGH-92
Later name(s):
Location: Adelaide, South Australia   Date: 1 October 2014
Comments:

Photographer: John Regan

Tug: WILLARA

Builder: Carrington Slipways, Newcastle

Engine: 2 x 6-cyl Niigata; 3600bhp

Propulsion: 2 x Z-peller units

Bollard pull: 47 tonnes

IMO: 8203127

Year built: 1983

Gross tonnage: 350

Former name(s): BLACKBURN COVE-83

Later name(s):

Location: Adelaide, South Australia   Date: 23 March 2016

Comments:

Photographer: John Southwood

Tug: TARPAN

Builder: Tamar Shipbuilding, Launceston

Engine: 2 x 6-cyl Daihatsu; 3600bhp

Propulsion: 2 x directional propellers

Bollard pull: 50 tonnes

IMO: 8317502

Year built: 1984

Gross tonnage: 426

Former name(s):

Later name(s):

Location: Adelaide, South Australia

Comments:

Photographer: John Regan

Date: 18 December 2012

Tug: WALAN
Builder: Tamar Shipbuilding, Launceston
Engine: 2 x 6-cyl Daihatsu; 3600bhp
Propulsion: 2 x fixed pitch propellers
Bollard pull: 45 tonnes
IMO: 8510893

Year built: 1986

Gross tonnage: 356

Former name(s): WALANA-97
Later name(s):
Location: Adelaide, South Australia
Comments:

Photographer: John Regan

Date: 18 December 2012

Tug: BULLARA

Builder: Nanindah, Batam

Engine: 2 x 6-cyl Daihatsu; 4830bhp

Propulsion: 2 x Z-peller units

Bollard pull: 61 tonnes

IMO: 9185621

Year built: 2000

Gross tonnage: 395

Former name(s):

Later name(s):

Location: Adelaide, South Australia

Comments:

Date: 23 March 2016

Photographer: John Southwood

Tug: TINGARI

Builder: Nanindah, Batam

Engine: 2 x 6-cyl Daihatsu; 4894bhp

Propulsion: 2 x Z-peller units

Bollard pull: 61 tonnes

IMO: 9185619

Year built: 2000

Gross tonnage: 395

Former name(s):

Later name(s):

Location: Adelaide, South Australia

Comments:

Photographer: John Southwood

Date: 27 March 2016

Tug: BURRA

Builder: Nanindah, Batam

Engine: 2 x 6-cyl Daihatsu; 4830bhp

Propulsion: 2 x Z-peller units

Bollard pull: 61 tonnes

IMO: 9185657

Year built: 2000

Gross tonnage: 395

Former name(s):

Later name(s):

Location: Adelaide, South Australia

Comments:

Photographer: John Regan

Date: 18 December 2012

Tug: SVITZER HERON

Builder: Jiangsu, Zhenjiang

Engine: 2 x 6-cyl Niigata; 4998bhp

Propulsion: 2 x Z-peller units

Bollard pull: 65 tonnes

IMO: 9578581

Year built: 2012

Gross tonnage: 442

Former name(s):

Later name(s):

Location: Adelaide, South Australia

Comments:

Date: 27 March 2016

Photographer: John Southwood

Tug: WOOREE

Builder: Carrington Slipways, Newcastle

Engine: 2 x 8-cyl Blackstone; 2440bhp

Propulsion: 2 x fixed pitch propellers

Bollard pull: 41 tonnes

IMO: 7606035

Year built: 1976

Gross tonnage: 266

Former name(s): BOTANY COVE-97

Later name(s):

Location: Port Pirie, South Australia   Date: 2 October 2014

Comments:

Photographer: John Regan

Tug: ELGIN

Year built: 1985

Builder: Elder Prince Marine Services, Fremantle

Engine: 2 x 8-cyl Alco; 3242bhp

Propulsion: 2 x fixed pitch propellers

Bollard pull: 42 tonnes

Gross tonnage: 267

IMO: 8740096

Former name(s):

Later name(s):

Location: Port Pirie, South Australia   Date: 19 December 2012

Comments: Reported sold in 2014 and working in Benoa, Indonesia, in 2017.

Photographer: John Regan

Tug: RIVERWIJS ISABELLE

Builder: Keppel Singmarine, Singapore

Engine: 2 x 6-cyl Niigata; 3198bhp

Propulsion: 2 x Z-peller units

Bollard pull: 43 tonnes

IMO: 9226310

Year built: 2000

Gross tonnage: 257

Former name(s):

Later name(s):

Location: Bunbury, Western Australia

Comments:

Photographer: John Regan

Date: 3 December 2014

Tug: WAMBIRI

Year built: 1986

Builder: Australian Shipbuilding Industries, Fremantle

Engine: 2 x 8-cyl Daihatsu; 4800bhp

Propulsion: 2 x Z-peller units

Bollard pull: 61 tonnes

Gross tonnage: 477

IMO: 8515518

Former name(s):

Later name(s):

Location: Henderson, Western Australia

Date: 29 January 2014

Comments:

Photographer: John Regan

Tug: SVITZER ALBATROSS   Year built: 2011
Builder: Jiangsu, Zhenjiang
Engine: 2 x 6-cyl Niigata; 4998bhp
Propulsion: 2 x Z-peller units
Bollard pull: 65 tonnes   Gross tonnage: 442
IMO: 9554315
Former name(s):
Later name(s):
Location: Henderson, Western Australia
Date: 21 May 2013
Comments:

Photographer: John Regan

Tug: SVITZER HARRIER   Year built: 2011
Builder: Jiangsu, Zhenjiang
Engine: 2 x 6-cyl Niigata; 4998bhp
Propulsion: 2 x Z-peller units
Bollard pull: 65 tonnes   Gross tonnage: 442
IMO: 9554327
Former name(s):
Later name(s):
Location: Henderson, Western Australia
Date: 21 May 2013
Comments:

Photographer: John Regan

Tug: STIRLING SKATE

Builder: Carrington Slipways, Newcastle

Engine: 2 x Detroit; 680bhp

Propulsion: 2 x fixed pitch propellers

Bollard pull: 14 tonnes

IMO: 6827981

Year built: 1968

Gross tonnage: 103

Former name(s): KURANDA-00

Later name(s):

Location: Fremantle, Western Australia   Date: 16 May 2012

Comments:

Photographer: John Regan

Tug: RIVERWIJS EDWINA

Year built: 1989

Builder: Australian Shipbuilding Industries, Fremantle

Engine: 2 x 9-cyl Deutz; 4840bhp

Propulsion: 2 x directional propellers

Bollard pull: 50 tonnes

Gross tonnage: 470

IMO: 8806981

Former name(s): COWRIE COVE-02

Later name(s): 14-SVITZER EDWINA

Location: Fremantle, Western Australia

Date: 26 February 2014

Comments:

Photographer: John Regan

Tug: SVITZER EAGLE   Year built: 2008
Builder: ASL, Singapore
Engine: 2 x 6-cyl Niigata; 4998bhp
Propulsion: 2 x Z-peller units
Bollard pull: 65 tonnes   Gross tonnage: 439
IMO: 9431070
Former name(s):
Later name(s):
Location: Fremantle, Western Australia
Date: 29 January 2012
Comments:

Photographer: John Regan

Tug: SVITZER FALCON   Year built: 2009
Builder: ASL, Singapore
Engine: 2 x 6-cyl Niigata; 4998bhp
Propulsion: 2 x Z-peller units
Bollard pull: 65 tonnes   Gross tonnage: 439
IMO: 9431082
Former name(s):
Later name(s):
Location: Fremantle, Western Australia
Date: 17 July 2013
Comments:

Photographer: John Regan

Tug: SVITZER MENJA

Builder: Baltijos, Klaipeda

Engine: 2 x 16-cyl Caterpillar; 5710bhp

Propulsion: 2 x directional propellers

Bollard pull: 73 tonnes

IMO: 9317896

Year built: 2005

Gross tonnage: 385

Former name(s):

Later name(s): SVITZER MYALL-10

Location: Lindø shipyard, Odense, Denmark   Date: 21 January 2008

Comments: Assisting EUGEN MÆRSK from the shipyard for trials.

Photographer: Bent Mikkelsen

On 10 March 2009, Svitzer tugs have the assistance of a tug from Kiel in easing the newly-built MATHILDE MÆRSK away from the Lindø shipyard at the mouth of Odense fjord. Launched on 29 January 2009, the container ship was about to undergo trials and she was handed over to her owners on 17 March.

(Bent Mikkelsen)

Pouring rain greeted the naming ceremony of the first three Svitzer M tugs at the Baltijos shipyard in Klaipeda on 15 May 2004. This is a rare photograph of SVITZER MJØLNER and SVITZER MILFORD under their original names as their identities were switched almost immediately. Tug #705 was initially named SVITZER MILFORD afloat in Klaipeda on 15 May and #706 was named SVITZER MJØLNER ashore. The accommodation in the first two units was too small, certainly too small for the cabins to be approved under the British flag. At this stage of build it would have been impossible or very expensive to alter the accommodation on tug #705 but it was possible on #706 and therefore Svitzer in the UK received the third instead of the second unit in the series. Thus what had been SVITZER MJØLNER became SVITZER MILFORD.

(Bent Mikkelsen)